# How to Start a Cleaning Business

## Make Your First $100,000 Using This Powerful Commercial Cleaning Business Model

**Maxwell Rotheray**

# Copyright



Printed in the United States of America
**© 2020 by Maxwell Rotheray**

ZeroNever Publishing House

USA | UK | Canada

# Table of Contents


Copyright................................................2

CHAPTER ONE:.................................5

Commercial cleaning business lucrative.......5

CHAPTER TWO:................................10

How to kick off in a Commercial Cleaning Business................................................10

CHAPTER THREE:.............................14

Why cleaning business could be profitable - Expected profit (short/long term analysis) .14

CHAPTER FOUR:...............................17

Expected profit in a house cleaning business ................................................................17

CHAPTER FIVE:.................................21

Commercial cleaning business checklist.....21

CHAPTER SIX:...................................26

How to target the right client.....................26

CHAPTER SEVEN:..............................34

Marketing your cleaning business..............34

CHAPTER EIGHT:..............................52

Pitfalls to avoid in cleaning business...........52

CHAPTER NINE: ...............................................61

How to expand/establish your brand ..........61

CHAPTER TEN:..................................................72

How to hire the right assistance .................72

CHAPTER ELEVEN: .......................................79

Best locations for cleaning business............79

CHAPTER TWELVE: ......................................85

Marketing tips...................................................85

# CHAPTER ONE:

# Commercial cleaning business lucrative

Many people don't like to be called cleaners, but then many people don't get paid to scrub floors and wash carpets and clean windows. The commercial cleaning business can be profitable, flexible, and can grow quickly, making it a great home business preference, if you key into the right path.

Professional Cleaning Business has the tendency of lower up-front costs than other businesses, and this is one of the few businesses you can begin working on immediately with little capital investment, so far you're willing to work hard for the initial aim of breaking even, and subsequently, make modest profit and eventually reasonable profit in the medium term.

With the exception of some specialized cleaning chemicals and equipment, most cleaning jobs will not be different from the products you use in your own household chores. Formal training or certifications are not necessarily required for typical home and office cleaning, but that doesn't mean a potential professional shouldn't undergo some kind of training if he hopes to get established in the business quickly. For those that have a high level of work ethic and customer demeanour, the cleaning business can be a lucrative and rewarding experience.

A friend or family member or other professional associates involved in the cleaning services industry will be a huge resource, but never mind if you are going into cleaning business for the first time even without knowing anybody. Ultimately, what you need to have a flourishing cleaning business is excellent service and a good number of satisfied customers.

The following are the reasons why you should try your hand in commercial cleaning business.

**i. Constant Market:** The janitorial industry is not known for the boom or bust wave that other markets are known for. Businesses need their offices cleaned whether in a good economy or bad one if it wants to keep a professional and clean environment. Commercial cleaning maintains a steady market with steady demand.

**ii. Simple Service Offering:** Most of the time every commercial house is in need of some type of janitorial services and offering this service is simple and can be provided by different kinds of people. Whether an entrepreneur decides to tap from an existing franchise model or build it from the scratch, what businesses need is fairly similar across the board such as emptying wastebaskets, cleaning bathrooms, dusting tables and chairs, washing toilets, and the typical sweeping and mopping.

**iii. Business Is Stable:** Commercial cleaning is a continuing service business. This means that companies and other businesses need the service regularly, which brings in steady business for you as well as a secure, regular income.

**iv. Entry-Level Workforce:** It is possible you can try to do all the work yourself; you'll find it more economical in terms of your time and income by hiring people to help you. The good thing about it is that your employees don't need formal education or training, so you don't have to spend money on expensive training or recruiting costs. Moreover, the greater part of the work is done after the offices are closed, so you can hire people who need evening schedules or want an additional job.

**v. Overhead is low:** Outside of cleaning supplies and other essentials, someone interested in a commercial cleaning franchise doesn't have to commit a lot of cash to buy cleaning equipment such as vehicles or inventory. In fact, it is possible to start this business without a vacuum or a car. With that mentioned, you'll want to invest in essential tools and equipment that will add value to your time and effort as your business gets underway.

# CHAPTER TWO:

# How to kick off in a Commercial Cleaning Business

1. Make up your mind if you want to start anew or you want to be a franchisee.

To start completely anew, you must be prepared for extra work, but it is possible on a lean budget. Franchises come with name recognition and a business plan, but there are usually conditions and can be expensive to procure. Also, you will decide whether it is going to be a one-man squad or will you need the services of others?

2. Take care of initial business start-up tasks:

These may include choosing a business name, putting in place a business structure, getting the business registered, and putting forward your initial business plan. If you wish to employ workers, you have to obtain an Employee Identification Number (EIN) from the IRS. It is absolutely free of charge, and besides, you will need to acquaint yourself with employment related laws.

3. Obtain relevant insurance and surety bonding.

4. Decide on your target market and your unique selling propositions:

Do you want to focus on specific businesses (such as commercial offices or residential houses) or maybe a specific section of your city? Things that can set you apart from others may include green cleaning (use of non-toxic products), price, and standard level of service.

5. Obtain the necessary tools, equipment and supplies.

You might be able to procure them wholesale at cleaning speciality stores. Items to have on your list may include cloths, disinfectant, air freshener, trash bags, broom, mop, vacuum, cleaners, and a carrying caddy. You would need equipment for each cleaning team if you need helpers.

6. Establish your pricing structure:

This may entail how you'll estimate bids, billing system, and drafting of contract agreements.

7. Print business cards, brochures/flyers, and other business documents.

8. Promote your business. Use your network via social media and personal contact, put an advertisement in local business media your target market reads, create a website if desired, have a sign on your vehicle, and any other marketing tactics that will help you let people know you are there.

9. Do a great job by asking for testimonials and/or referrals to grow your business faster.

# CHAPTER THREE:

# Why cleaning business could be profitable -Expected profit (short/long term analysis)

## Cleaning business profit potential

How much does a cleaning business make per year as profit?

The cleaning business profit potential is first-rate on the peak-end of the range. Cleaning business profits can run a range from low earning income to top-earning income. Results vary a great deal. Cleaning business earning potential is largely dependent by your market focus and your ability to create business systems that deliver services to that market. Drawing a business plan for your cleaning service is fundamental in determining this.

**Cleaning Business Profit Potential**

Your cleaning business profit potential depends largely on scale and complexity. With residential cleaning, your overhead and other incidental expenses can be quite low, but in the commercial cleaning sphere they can be quite high, the difference lies in the equipment necessary to do the job and the degree of service that is required and its associated up-front costs. For instance, lone squad cleaner cleaning an apartment has very little indirect cost and expense because you can even use the clients cleaning solutions and vacuum, but if you are going to clean a production facility (with an office attached) you will procure a floor polisher, steam machine, and a vehicle to transport both equipment and workers.

## Commercial Sector Cleaning Profits

Commercial sector cleaning profits are higher overall than residential as a result of primarily to unrestricted scaling and built-in higher profits due to the necessity of the service and the scale of the market, including the risks involved. It can be complicated to scale an apartment cleaning company because you can only clean so many houses in a day and there is a ceiling on what one house will cost to clean. The regularity of cleaning is usually shorter and many customers in the market create a low ball estimate effect across the conventional market. In other words, a bad cleaning with your home will be unsatisfactory but it will not have an effect on you beyond that, but commercial cleaning failure can have devastating consequences for the business or professional organization, so there is less emphasis on saving money as a priority with commercial cleaning.

# CHAPTER FOUR:

## Expected profit in a house cleaning business

Having an idea of your potential profit margin when going into a house cleaning business is vital not only for managing the company but also to make up your mind whether you can function gainfully. The profit margin is the percentage relationship between net income and sales. Revenue is the gross amount of money the business earns by cleaning houses. Net income is your gross income less any expenses. The profit margin indicates what per cent of every dollar in revenue that is actually profit.

**Calculating Revenue**

For simplicity sake, we'll take the example of cleaning just two houses. Let's suppose that it takes one employee ten hours to clean the two houses, and we can charge $150 for each house for the service. What you are expected to charge will be based on the size of the houses you are cleaning, the amount of competition in the area and the demand for house cleaning. In this example, our takings are $300.

## Calculating Expenses

We now need to gather and calculate all the expenses the business incurred while cleaning the house. If you pay your employee $15 per hour, that's $150 in payroll expenses. If you're also reimbursing for gas, that will be an extra expense that depends on the distance driven--let's suppose for this job it was $5. Many cleaning services request that customers supply their own cleaning products. If your enterprise operates this way, the remaining expense you have to incur is the insurance. This expense depends on various factors. We will overlook it for now and calculate our expenses to be $155.

## Calculating Profit Margin

The profit margin is net income divided by takings. Net income is our takings, $300, minus our expenses, $155. In this case, our net income is $145. When we divide net income by takings, we come to a profit margin of 48 per cent approx. If you have incurred greater expenses or have lower takings, your profit margin will be lower.

**Putting Everything Together**

A profit margin of 48 per cent means that for every dollar our house cleaning business earns, 48 cents is profit. This is a very strong profit margin. If you want to take the insurance expense into account, you must divide your monthly insurance cost by the total number of houses you clean in one month and add this to our total expense number above. Keep in mind that this is the profit margin after we have paid any initial startup expenses and not the capital expenditure--like the purchase of a vacuum, steam machine or carpet cleaner. The capital expenditure is a fixed asset and only their annual use (depreciation) is considered when calculating profit. House cleaning businesses tend to have low startup costs and high-profit margins.

# CHAPTER FIVE:

# Commercial cleaning business checklist

The business plan is the starting point of your checklist when you are setting up a cleaning business. Find out who are the key actors you will be competing with, their marketing strategies in terms of services they offer, their advertising strategy and their pricing method. Also, determine whether you want to be a one-man squad or you want to engage employees to administer the cleaning. Decide whether you want to work under a license from an established business, or start your cleaning business from scratch. Additionally, approximate how much capital you will need and how your cleaning business will be funded.

## Supplies and Equipment

You will need to procure certain supplies and equipment for your cleaning business, such as mops, brooms, a vacuum cleaner, trash bags, floor and glass cleaners, squeegees, spray bottles and cleaning cloths. You should also decide from the onset if at all you want to be in the business of cleaning carpets and scrubbing floors with a floor scrubbing machine. If you decide to go into commercial cleaning, then you can rent carpet-cleaning or floor-polishing machines as when they are required. By renting a variety of machines for the cleaning jobs, your initial expenses will be low.

## Licenses and Insurance

File an application to procure a vendor's license at your local city hall or county administration office. All your takings will be subject to taxes. Moreover, you should register your business as a DBA (doing business as) via the same local government office. A DBA is typically essential if you have a name for your business. You may also be required by your State to procure other licenses and permits. You may require some liability insurance for your cleaning business, in accordance with Entrepreneur.com. Liability insurance will protect you from potential lawsuits in cases where people are injured because of the materials you use in scrubbing the floor. For instance, people may fall on wet floors or develop respiratory problems from chemicals you use to clean the floors. The Occupational Safety and Health Administration also has its restrictions, you may have to sight its list of requirements for cleaning businesses at OSHA.gov.

**Target Market**

Decide on your target market, whether you want to target consumers or businesses. Consumer clients are mainly owners and renters of homes, apartments and condominiums. Businesses are mainly office complexes, hospitals, schools, libraries and corporations. Target small office complexes in your area if you want to focus on business clients. Start making contact with companies like Molly Maid if you want to buy a residential cleaning franchise. Think about those who offer franchising like Jani-King and Coverall if you want to be in the commercial cleaning business. If you opt for franchising, you have to sign a detailed contract with the franchisor and make sure you comply with the agreement.

**Promotion**

Determine the type of advertising tools you will use to disseminate information for your cleaning business. Print and distribute flyers to residential customers in your community. Visit business outfits and leave a business card and brochure with them, and try to be more professional with business owners in your approach. In addition, some business owners' requirements are that you submit a bid for jobs. If the budget permits, advertise your cleaning business in the print and online yellow pages as well as running ads in various coupon magazines that are distributed to residences.

# CHAPTER SIX:

# How to target the right client

Attracting clients for your cleaning service

Starting a commercial cleaning service is a splendid way to have a home-based business going, and it does not need a lot of startup funding. To achieve the success you need clients who will always hire you. Acquiring clients for your cleaning service business does not have to be too hard. If you decide to offer a perfect and reliable service at a reasonable price, you will always have individuals and companies wanting to hire you. Getting clients for a commercial/residential cleaning service is by increasing your visibility, asking for referrals from satisfied customers and offering coupons and discounts. Others are:

a. Satisfied customers - these are the most effective sources of contacts

b. Endless chain   -   Make an attempt to secure at least one additional contact from each person you interview.

c. Centre of influence   -   You should join organizations or participate in activities where you can meet and interact with influential people who may provide contact information.

d. Spotters   -   persuade ordinary working people (such as retail clerks, non-competing salespeople)   to   provide   you   with information.

e. Networking   -   Try and use a personal relationship with those who are connected and willing to assist to secure contact information.

f. Promotional activities   -   Use the opportunities provided by the internet to make inquiries, advertise and send direct mail, visit trade shows, and seminars to secure contact information.

g. Lists and directories  - You should make use of secondary data sources, which can be free or fee-based.

h. Cold canvassing   - Visit companies in a promising neighbourhood or calling people listed in the telephone book to uncover contact information.

j. Trade fairs and exhibitions  - Visit and explain your services at trade shows or exhibitions where interested people tend to gather (Human Resources Managers for instance)is a way to acquire many names and addresses for later follow-up sales calls or mailings.

k. Observations  -  be alert to changes or events in your territory that might affect your business, reading newspapers, watching T.V programmes are one way to find leads

l. Seminars -  Organise seminars where you give useful information to attendees and collect their contact addresses.

**So how can you break through to new clients? As a starting point, try these five tips:**

Create a marketing plan. Making you visible in your community will attract clients to your cleaning service.

- Print flyers, postcards, business cards and other materials that explain your business and offer contact information. You can send them out, hand them out or post them to places where business solicitations are permitted.
- Advertise whenever possible. Your business might profit from print ads in your community newspaper or free online ads on sites such as Craigslist. Radio 2
- List yourself in the Yellow Pages and other community directories and phone books. Many people turn to these places when they need a solution, so you want to make sure you are there under "cleaning service

Advertisements can also be affordable and easy to produce.

- Ask for referrals. If you have secured your first or more clients who are happy with the cleaning services you provide, ask them to recommend you to their contacts.
- Look to your own network for referrals. Ask for help from friends, family, neighbours, other business associates and social groups.
- Invite friends and clients to "like" or "follow" your social networking pages. This is a great way to build your base of potential clients.
- Promote your cleaning services with coupons and discounts. People love saving money, and a great coupon or special price will get the attention of potential customers.
- Put forward a handsome discount for the first cleaning service.
- Offer discounts to clients who refer you to other clients. Giving your current

clients for new business incentives will keep them happy and provide them with great motivation to recommend you.

- Increase/refocus your advertising. Is your business taking advantage of social media and online advertising? For basic coverage on advertising in the Internet age, you need to be present on the internet, even having your own website.
- Sell more services to current clients. Do you have an opportunity to up-sell additional cleaning services to your current clients?
- Network with connected businesses. Say you run a commercial cleaning business. It would be great to get to know the janitorial companies, window cleaners, and another trade-in your area. Many small-business entrepreneurs refer customers who need services they do not offer.
- Think local. Take an active part in your community affairs and local groups, it can help you establish connections.

Give attention to your professional image. As part of attracting new clients, it is also making a good impression.

- Wear uniform or clean clothes that fit well – be smart. While you are providing a cleaning service doesn't mean you will be dirty, you do not want to show up looking sloppy or untidy.
- Keep your vehicle clean and maintained as well. If you have people who work for you, make sure they maintain a standard way of dressing and image requirements.

Create a professional network. The more people you exposed to, the more you are able to promote your business and gain new clients.

- Join your local Chamber of Commerce. Look for other opportunities with local business groups as well.

Become bonded and insured. This will give your business extra credibility, and it will help you ease any concerns people might have about allowing strangers in their homes.

Build a good reputation. It will be hard to attract clients if you do not offer a great service that supersedes one of the competitors for a reasonable price.

- Request for evaluations periodically. Leave surveys for your clients to complete, or check-in via email to make sure they are satisfied. You can use any positive remarks as testimonials.
- Attend quickly to any complaints or concerns once it develops.

# CHAPTER SEVEN:

# Marketing your cleaning business

i. Brand your business

ii. Communicate your differential advantage

iii. Create an exceptional customer experience

iv. Get a professional logo/uniform

v. Get a business website

vi. Create your business Facebook page

vii. After your first excellent job, keep doing an awesome job

viii. Ask for Referrals in the Right Way

ix. Motivate your prospective clients

x. Turn Your Car into a Rolling Billboard

xi. Use door-to-door tactics to drop Flyers

XII. Direct Mail, Door Hangers, and Flyers:

XIII. Build an (Invisible) Email Selling Machine

XIV. Get Your Website to the Front Page (SEO)

XV. Getting Great Online Reviews (and Deal with the Bad Ones)

## I. Brand your business

A brand is a combination of name, symbol, sign, and design which clearly identifies one product/service from another. Branding indeed is about the following:

- It is about what your values are as a cleaning company

- What you believe in as a cleaning company

- The experience you want your customers to have when you clean their offices

- What makes your cleaning business different from others?

- What makes your cleaning outfit rank better than competitors (competitive advantage)

By branding your service, you have set your service quality apart from competitors.

## II. Communicate your differential advantage

You must set out how to promote what actually set you apart from competitors (Unique Selling Propositions). Once you identify what makes you different from competitors, you must communicate the same to your prospective clients. It might be:

- Friendly cleaning fluids you use to clean

- Thorough cleaning work you do

- Rapid response to emergency

- Cleaning work that is done at add hours

## III. Create an exceptional customer experience

Give your customers what you believe in and what are your values. If your values and that is what you believe in, then offer the same to your customers. Be consistent with this so that each job you carry out stands out excellently. If the experience you want to offer your customers are on the basis of protecting the environment, and then part of the experience you could offer your customers is eco-friendly cleaning in which you use green cleaning products. This means that people that are on the side of protecting the environment will choose you over a competitor that does not do this.

## IV. Create a professional logo/uniform

Try to make your business easily recognized by prospective customers. Make a logo that identifies your cleaning outfit. When people see your logo, they easily identify what your company can do. Also, dress smart, together with your workers. When you put on your working uniform, you are advertising your business. People who don't know you will ask questions and find out.

## V. Create your business website

Your website is your office in the space. It means that anybody from anywhere can access your site and read about you and your services. It is not about having a website; it is about driving visitors to the site so that they will learn about what you do. So you must design a good interactive website and use any available tactics including social media to drive traffic to the site. Don't forget to use a website professional for the design.

Digital marketing is the most powerful form of marketing today. In a study carried out in 2015, over 80% of consumers use online search before deciding to make a purchase.

The use of this internet marketing strategies guarantees that your business will be discovered first by those who search for cleaning services.

Use them to generate more clients for your cleaning business on demand. They go hand-in-hand with great SEO on your website.

## VI. Create your business Facebook page

Use social media personnel to create the page and get people to like the page beginning with family members, friends, and business associates.

## VII. After Your First Job, Keep Doing an Awesome job

Above all other marketing strategies, keep doing a fantastic job

When you make the quality for your clients a priority, your client will:

• Think like they're getting value for money

• Be more disposed to recommend you to others

• Keep coming back to you, again and again!

The cost of acquiring new clients far outweighs the cost of retaining existing ones. So make your cleaning services themselves your first marketing tactic.

## VIII. Ask for Referrals in the Right Way

Word of mouth is one of the most excellent ways to get great, enduring clients. Referrals work because they can double-cross you past new clients'"trust barrier."

But it can be tough – and even a little frightening – to ask for referrals.

The following are some of the successful tricks to make your requests:

i. Choose the right clients to make the request to

• From your best clients, determine the most perfect.

• Determine the most loyal to you.

• Determine the most friendly of all.

Which client has been with you for the longest time, and is interested in buying more of your services?

ii. Choose the right time to strike (Ask)

• The most excellent time to ask for referrals (like asking for online reviews) is when your client is most thrilled about you.

• That means, right after you have displayed the best job you've ever done for them. Give it above 100 per cent next time you service a client and try asking for a referral.

## IX.     Motivate your prospective clients

• You should have a gift card policy that works.

• The general idea is that you offer a referral "gift card" to clients. They can give the gift card to a friend or family member of his choice, so that person gets $25 off his first service. When someone is excited about your work, go ahead and ask. Remember: "if you don't ask, you don't get."

## X. Turn Your Car into a Rolling Billboard

On a daily basis, 40,000 to 60,000 people will see your car, on average. That sounds huge of potential clients. There are several ways available to wrap your company vehicle. The bottom line is this: If you choose a high quality adn your car, for longevity, go with a car wrap. If you just want something that will get you exposed for now with as little money as possible, get some custom-built magnet clings.

Make sure to add your:

• Logo

• Phone number

• Website or Blog

Add something that reverberates the benefits of your services.

You don't want to put a long list of your services on your car. They could be confusing, and nobody really is interested in reading them.

## XI. Use door-to-door tactics to drop flyers

You may not want to stuff your marketing pieces into the mailbox ... together with all other unsolicited mail from financial institutions and credit card companies? Be assured that door-to-door flyers still work!

There are some distribution methods to select for this purpose:

• Pay an employee to walk around neighbourhoods (the cost can be very high)

• Pay a third party to walk around neighbourhoods (works great if you trust your third party)

• Get your employees to distribute your flyers door-to-door in the neighbourhood they work.

Your prospective clients will see your flyer on their door, and also see your car parked across the street... So your name sticks in their heads. This also gives them the green light to go and talk to their neighbours, and enquire about how good your services are.

## XII.    Targeted Mail and Leaflets:

Establish Extra Cleaning Sales. The fact is that you can put all of these in one category.

The process requires three steps to carry out any Targeted Mail or Door Hanger/Flyer blitz.

1. Generate

2. Hand out

3. Test and improve

**Step 1: Create**

Like any marketing tool, there are a number of elements you need to include in your marketing piece.

• The name of your Company

• Your identity as the answer to your target's predicament

• How to contact you

But the most important part of your marketing piece is the Offer, which should be so juicy nobody can resist.

• Perhaps you offer a 50% one-time cleaning service with every deep clean.

• Or maybe, you give "one quarter off" on every customer introduced?

**Step 2: Distribute**

Print Marketing is expensive. You must shun some ostensible huge errors when crafting your targeted mail.

Here's what most cleaning business owners are not aware of: the most expensive part of Print Marketing is not printing out the flyers and postcards... The true cost is in the distribution.

**How to Execute Direct Mail**

Basically, what is required is using compatible software to choose a few houses in a particular area, gather their contact details, and mail them your postcards directly.

This works better for two reasons:

• You can target a neighbourhood where a large number of your ideal clients live

• You can build route density in a small area, to keep your routes tight and save several hours on drive time

**XIII. Create a sales person in the form of Email Selling Machine**

So far, the strategies have been to attracting potential customers to your business. But what happens when someone doesn't buy on first sight?

 It's all about the follow-up. 95% of people don't buy on their first visit... so you need a way to keep them coming back.

Email marketing is flourishing because it rings a bell to your clients that you still function and you can still be a solution to their problems.

• First step is to write the emails.

• Next you step up an Email Marketing "Machine." You need to set up a series of emails (or an email campaign) to send to your clients over a set period of time.

It delivers outstanding results if you apply specific interest segmentation. Are clean windows of interest to them?  Gleaming tile? You can follow all these automatically with the exact software, via an easy-to-use tag system.

There are diverse tools in the market to execute sending emails out in batches. But if you really want to segment your leads and up-sell your clients for maximum effect, look at Service Autopilot.

This software lets you put tag on leads and clients, subdivide them, and robotically send them emails on the basis of what services that have previously (or have not) been delivered to them.

## XIV. Make Your Website easy to be seen (SEO)

Search Engine Optimization, or SEO, puts your website on the top of search results, because the higher your page ranks, the more visitors you will get.

SEO is about two things:

• Informing Search Engines what your pages are about

• Offering your users the greatest experience possible

It's a vast and complicated topic, but critical to cleaning business owners because of your local competition.

## XV. Getting GREAT Online Reviews (and Deal with the Bad Ones)

The more reviews you get, the better for your business. Online reviews are the new way people "sample" your business before they hire you. The more first-class reviews you have, the more likely people will be disposed to hire your services.

To get a 5-star review is amazingly simple. It is about three simple steps:

• Request for reviews from your loyal clients.

• Mail them or leave them a note. Don't forget you only make your request when they are in an excellent state of mind with you (i.e. after you've satisfied them in your job).

• Say thank you to anyone who leaves you a great review.

You should respond to all of your reviews. Respond to your negative reviews in the best possible way. Move the discussion out of the public eye once you notice it.Leave a message for them. Ask them to mail or call you. Promise to fix any problem they have with your service ASAP. Do whatever is necessary to get them to reverse their review to 4 or 5 star.

**The Most Important Places to Get Online Reviews for Your Cleaning Business:**

1. Google (This will make an excellent difference on your SEO.)

2. Facebook

3. Yelp

4. Angle's List

5. Thumbtack (and other similar sites.)

Never fake any accounts. You can ask real friends and family members to leave reviews, but faking accounts will ruin your business.

# CHAPTER EIGHT:

## Pitfalls to avoid in cleaning business

While starting your cleaning business, don't take the risks of making these 8 common mistakes:

1. Not tell everyone that needs to be told

2. Not distributing flyers enough.

3. Not creating a "professional" website.

4. Not giving estimates for every job.

5. Not making notes for every job.

6. Not treating your cleaning business seriously from your very first day.

7. Not having realistic expectations.

8. Not taking corrections from both your cleaning & interpersonal skills.

**I. Tell everyone that needs to be told**

Once you have decided to go into commercial cleaning, take steps toward building your new cleaning business, tell everyone who needs to be told. Begin by sharing the news of your new business with everybody you know: you don't know who will bring you the first business. Begin to spread the news with your friends, your spouse, your parents and all your aunts and your siblings. People are always glad to hear about a new business. Mail out to people in your group of friends, such as your buddy who led your group in sports at school, and your former college friends who are holding positions in government and industry, and ask them to spread the news in their groups. Remember to use good, old-fashioned grassroots social networking to get the word across.

**II. Distribute Flyers every day.**

Distribute fliers every day. If you don't have a daytime job, go out for upward of three hours each day and distribute flyers for your new cleaning business. Just put one foot in front of the other and work to see your business take shape in no time. If you are engaged during the day, then distribute flyers for one hour in the evening after work. It is possible that distributing flyers is not everyone's favourite thing to do but it works so well and gets good results so quickly when it is properly done. Engaging someone else may not guarantee it is well done. When your phone starts buzzing and traffic to your cleaning business website is increasing by the day, you'll know your efforts at hitting the sidewalk are paying off. Aside from growing your business quickly, distributing flyers has a special bonus. You will feel good after getting some exercise. In addition, you'll learn about the nooks and cranny of neighbourhoods where you want to work.

### III. Use your Cleaning Business Website.

Your website is your office in the market space and a major source of information about your cleaning business, irrespective of the fact whether you are working, resting or whiling away time with friends. Make the best use of your website's capabilities. Make sure your website address is prominently displayed so that it is easy for people who pick up your flyer to check out your cleaning business online. Be ready to offer special coupons and cleaning guidelines on your site to engage people and feed them with useful information. When someone makes enquiry through your website, respond promptly and courteously. Provide them with reasons to remember you. Never forget how powerful word-of-mouth advertising can be, and how swift it can go online.

## IV. Practice giving estimates.

Just as in sports and every aspect of life endeavour it takes time to be a master of anything you do, practice makes perfect. Learn how to give estimates for your cleaning jobs and your skills will be improved quickly. Practice role-playing at a friend's house. Knock on their front door and when they answer the door, introduce yourself and be prepare to be invited into their home or place of business. Find out about their needs and take notes of the conversation. Take down your impressions of the conditions of their rooms. You must take note of things like the number of furniture in each room (they have to be dusted). Is there enough space? Are there some fragile items that have to be treated with special care? Everyone you do an estimate for is different, and their "stuff" is not the same. Keep your eyes wide open and learn. Practice giving estimates so you will be more relaxed and self-confident and you'll get more jobs sooner than you think.

**V. Keep notes.**

Take your notebook, your android phone, your tablet, (or whatever you've got!) to every estimate you give, and every job you're on. You may think that you'll remember when Ms Jones asks you to arrive one hour early next time and clean the cooker and fridge. But you are busy. Don't make yourself look foolish and don't take the risk of disappointing your clients and losing them eventually. Take notes instead. Make this a routine, a part of your policy. Systems are only really helpful when they are applied. It doesn't matter what type of system you use, just use one that works to hold it fast. That way, you won't lose business and you won't waste time trying to remember the response you gave the last client the previous day.

## VI. Treat your cleaning business like a regular job.

What gives joy to a cleaner is to bring home the money at the end of the day, especially when you know that you have put in your best to earn it. Embarking on a cleaning business is just like any business in its infancy stages. You have to work hard to get the outcome you want to see. We're also very thrilled to show you how to get where you want to be, in your business. However, no one but you alone can decide how motivated you are. Treat your new business with respect to the respect of a new wife. Put in the time and the effort it needs to get off the ground and rolling in the early days. Shortly, you'll gaze back and appreciate that YOU are the one that made it all come to pass. It's a wonderful feeling.

Take care of your new business as if it is your regular job from the outset. Put in 8-hour days or more and hang to it until you reach your goals. You will be able to relax into the job, and yes, even coast at it, eventually. But first things first, you must gain knowledge of and internalize all your new skills and experiences, pending when they become second nature.

## VII. Have realistic expectations.

Your cleaning business will, as a matter of fact, take some time and effort to be up and running. You already have an idea. So keep the focus on your goals, and follow the steps. A business will begin to roll in from distributing flyers and from other advertising tools you have used to spread the news, such as your business website, but you might have to take things easy and be patient at first. You are building up a worthwhile business, and it must take shape via stages of development, growth, and then maturity. Don't forget that people who are in need of a cleaning service often have your flyer for weeks or even months before they decide to call you. Most of the time, something will have to trigger it; either their current cleaner misbehaved in the job or left for any reason before they decide to give you a trial. Some people will call you almost immediately, while others will keep your flyer in view because someone else is doing the job. Your marketing efforts will eventually earn you a dividend in both long-term and short-term scenarios.

## VIII. Practice your 'people skills'

Do you feel at ease just talking to people in an informal sort of way, such as, "Hey there, what do you think about those Fraudsters?" It is like you have a little fair to excellent people skills already. By "people skills" it is about pleasant and direct communication. People engaging a cleaning pro are usually looking for someone who they feel can carry out the job well, be trustworthy, and be easy to do business with. Practice on your \people skills' if you think they're a little out of form. It's a good idea to work towards being conversant with 'people skill'.

# CHAPTER NINE:

## How to expand/establish your brand

Many small-business owners are always pushing to find new business and sign new cleaning contracts. Naturally, it has to be so. However, many commercial businesses already have cleaners, so they can be slow to hire someone new. Some businesses have a low budget on cleaning and maintenance, so how can you as a cleaning company breakthrough into new clients and grow your business

No matter what size your cleaning business is, you definitely dream of growing it into something bigger. Growing your cleaning business will take a lot of hard work, but you can use the following tips to grow your business and reach your goal over time.

As a starting point, try the following guidelines:

## 1. Find a compatible niche

The cleaning industry has a lot of niches. Find the one that go with your interests and skills so you can make a difference from other cleaning services. For instance, you may want to market yourself as an eco-conscious company that uses cleaning liquids that are environmentally friendly, which means using organic cleaning products. Or, you may want to emphasize your willingness to provide extra services like keeping the premises tidy.

## 2. Always pursue new leads

You need new customers to expand your business, so you always have to track new leads. Some useful ways to generate new leads include:

• Using online media to connect with potential clients

• Picking up contact information on a regular basis from forms completed on your website

• Cold calling on businesses in your area

• Distributing flyers in your local community

## 3. Reward word-of-mouth referrals

Word-of-mouth marketing is credible and it is working because people trust the views of their friends, family members and colleagues.

Give incentives to your clients when they pass on information about your cleaning service to someone. You can allow them a discount to encourage them and show your appreciation. Even a small reward will encourage people to talk about you and promote your business.

## 4. Keep your clients happy

You devote time and energy to attract new clients. A little extra effort to keep them smiling is a welcome investment. By so doing, you would hardly lose them to competitors. A few nice ways to do this include:

• Checking in with them or at least calling them on the phone regularly to make sure they're happy with your services

• Sending them updates about your services

• Offering coupons or discounts for loyalty

• Sending them birthday wishes

• Offering them hampers during festivities, such as Christmas.

## 5. Disengage from customers that harm your business

As you gain new clients, you may discover that some of your old ones don't fit into your growth plan. The point is that you cannot serve a customer at all cost. Perhaps they pay lower rates that you charged when you first started your business and they want to continue on that basis, or they want you to provide services that you don't want to offer anymore. Or it maybe they don't like settling their bills and always fall behind. When you now discover that you don't want a customer anymore, sever ties so you can focus on new clients that will move your business forward.

## 6. Train your employees all round

As your business matures, you will have confidence in your employees to carry out their jobs without much supervision. If you give them the appropriate training, then they will be equipped with the skills to clean homes, offices and other areas as well as you can. Spend time brushing up employees on any cleaning secrets that you use to keep clients happy. They will be grateful for the knowledge gained and this appreciation will show in their work and devotion to your business.

## 7. Take care of your employees' welfare

It takes the investment of resources to find and train employees. Once you have a group of trustworthy people on your staff, treat them well so they don't dump you to work for competitors. Depending on your budget, you may want to take care of your employees by:

• Offering them superior benefits

• Giving them annual salary increases

• Rewarding them for exceptional performance.

## 8. Optimize your website

Using some basic search engine optimization (SEO) skills will assist you to get better search engine positions. Some of the majority of significant strategies rely on:

• Meta descriptions and title tags

• Local keywords

• Incoming links

• Internal links

• Evergreen content

## 10. Update your business plan

As your cleaning company grows, you will require upgrading and re-defining your strategies to keep it accurate and realistic. Ideally, you should review your business plans once in a month to fine-tune it as needed. An annual update can deal with bigger topics like diversifying into new markets and taking on new business trends.

## 11. Always innovate

Spend time brooding over innovative ways you can develop your business. Are there new services or styles you can use to make your offerings more efficient? Should you change to a subscription form instead of billing by the hour? Can you use modern tools to get in touch with your clients better?

Other cleaning companies are adjusting to new technologies to compete favourably. If you don't follow suit, then they will move on faster than you while stealing your clients.

## 12. Charge the right price

A lot of cleaning businesses appear to undervalue their services. If you don't your prices right because they are too low, then you will be lacking in revenue to grow your business. Instead of engaging in price war as a strategy to attack your opponents, top your services with extra value, and your clients will not mind paying more.

## 13. Re-invest in your business

As part of your growth strategy is the need to plough back profits into the company. If you want to grow, then you will need to spend money on:

• New scrubbing equipment

• Vehicles and vehicle repairs

• Improved branding

• Staff training

## 14. Use software to stay organize and up-to-date

Getting your business to stay organized gets harder as your business grows. Cleaning business software will help you plan services, sort out clients bills and trail expenses. If you begin using software then you will be able to manage your time well.

## 15. Protect yourself with insurance

Bad luck could put your company out of business. Insurance takes you out from financial pressures as a result by things such as:

• Employee costs

• Damage to vehicles

• Damage to fixed assets

As your business expands, the more important insurance is to your business. Assess your options so you can select a policy that gives you your business protection.

Cleaning business operates in a competitive environment, but you can still make your company successful. If you can go along with the tips, then you will always have a competitive advantage over your rivals in your area.

Here are some other marketing tips that can help grow your cleaning business:

1.      Get your business listed for free in local information bank (e.g., Yelp, Google My Business, Yahoo! Local Listings).

2.      Maintain an online presence on Facebook and Twitter.

3.     Always include important contact info (e.g., email, phone, website) on your marketing material such as flyers.

4.     Pretend to be small and publicize your business in local newspapers and websites.

5.     Be constant with your company name, logo, design, and colours across all platforms.


6. Publicize that your company is "bonded" if you have Surety/Contract Bonds that protect your clients.  (Remember that as your business expands, you might need to upgrade small business insurance coverage. More income implies more assets you have to protect, which means new or updated policies to deal with your cleaning contract liability and property damage risk.

# CHAPTER TEN:

# How to hire the right assistance

You may have started your cleaning company at the time you have a full-time job elsewhere. So as the business grew you could quit your "day job" and put more time into the cleaning business. Over time as the cleaning business grows you may find you can no longer manage all the tasks, you need to handle, no matter how much time you allocate to it. If you do not have time to market your business or to keep in contact with your clients regularly, it may be an appropriate time to bring in an employee. Engaging an employee helps you not only to keep your cleaning business growing but also allows you to have time to yourself.

**I.     List out the everyday jobs required in the cleaning business**

Begin your recruitment process by listing out the tasks needed in your cleaning business and then make up your mind on those you want (or need) Your first recruit should be more than just someone who will directly assist you but someone who will be able to help you with the overall growth of your cleaning business by helping not only with cleaning everyday jobs but by making sure they provide great customer service.

As you begin the hiring process, choose the job title and prepare an all-inclusive job description. This will assist you to centre on the responsibilities you want your employees to have, and then when you recruit your first worker, he or she will know what the scope of his or her duties are.

## II.    Personnel specification or man profile

This refers to the personal characteristics required to do a job eg skill; experience and special aptitudes.   Personnel specification would show the following:

Sex, age and physical characteristics required, e.g size, energy level , mental abilities and emotional maturity, cultural requirements e.g speech experience and skills needed.

**Means of job evaluation**

As well as a job description, you must find a way of evaluating job performance. You should provide a written evaluation regularly. In the course of the first year of employment you may want to evaluate at 3 months, 6 months, and finally at the end of the year. In subsequent years, job performance evaluations are usually done annually on the employee's employment anniversary date. If an employee is falling behind in doing a task, you must urgent steps to correct the situation.

**III.     Hiring the right staff**

Hiring the right person takes time. Set realistic goals for when you want that first person on board. It may take longer than a week or two to place an advertisement, interview and engage the right person. As you interview potential candidates, look for individuals who are eager and willing to do the job. You will put in place a training program to train most of the specific skills an employee will need. If you discover someone who has the right approach, don't ignore them if they have never scrub a floor before, or use carpet steamer or backpack vacuum.

Is your employee covered by your insurance? Find out with your insurance agent to be sure your employee is covered by your policy. Also since you are an employer, you'll need to provide workers compensation insurance. Your agent should be able to advise rightly in this area.

**IV.    Do have an employee manual and keep it up-to-date**

Your employee manual will cover areas such as the direction, assessments, time off procedures, tools policies, and the overall working responsibilities that your employees will have. It may also be in addition to data on safety - or the safety document may be separate. All of your policies should be documented before your employee's resume work the first time.

Nearly all your cleaning employees will be working in buildings at odd hours, so you will need to conduct thorough background checks before engagement. Your clients may decide not to conduct a background checks of your employees, but it is an indication of goodwill and added selling proposition for your business to let any potential customers recognize that you have gone the extra mile to have all your employees go through a background check prior to engagement.

**V. Have a training program in place.**

The training program should include how to execute general tasks that you expect your new employee to complete. Moreover, since your cleaning employees will be working with chemicals and equipment, they need to have specific training to deal with safety issues and to comply with OSHA standards.

## VI. Enlist with your state's employment department.

All states have a system in place for unemployment compensation. Employers are required to register the State and disburse into this fund through unemployment compensation taxes.

## VII. Use the payroll system

Put in place a payroll system that takes care of the withholding taxes and making payroll tax payments to the IRS. Work with your accountant to be sure you file the required paperwork.

It is the requirement of every employer to post specific labour notices at the worksite. The listing of the Federal posters you need to post have been put up on the Department of Labor's website. Visit your State department of labor for more details.

# CHAPTER ELEVEN:

# Best locations for cleaning business

Selecting a business location for your cleaning business is a significant aspect of your start-up to-do list. For you to choose a good location there are a number of factors you should take into account, the most important of which we'll try to analyze in this e-book. However, before going ahead and selecting a location, make sure you verify that your cleaning business is in accord with the special zoning regulations that may apply there. In this case, consult the local authorities for this matter.

What's obvious in a cleaning business is that you WILL have to go to your customers to carry out the cleaning services. Moreover, no matter what type of cleaning services you'll be offering, you will have to journey distances in order to do your job. As a general rule, you must make sure your business is rather close to your customers if not, you'll spend time and money travelling to and from your customers' location and back to your office. More so as your business develops and you're getting more cleaning contracts, having to travel long distances may not be cost-effective.

## Choosing a Business Location for House Cleaning Services

If you choose to start a cleaning business, you should make sure you're close to city population centres and have easy access by walking or driving to your customers. In this instance, running a home-based business rather than acquiring an office space may be the best way to go about it in terms of overhead costs and overall convenience. However, most residential areas cannot be used for commercial businesses. You may have to consult the local authorities to find out as there might be tight restrictions and zone regulations in place. You must also consider whether you will be engaging employees in the future, because if you do, running a home-based cleaning business is probably not the ideal thing to do.

## Choosing a Business Location for Commercial Cleaning Services

When choosing a business location for your commercial cleaning services, there's a great number of things you'll have to consider. To begin with, the ideal thing is that you will be hiring employees, if not in the short term, it is going to happen in the long term. Moreover, determine if you'll also be having customers come to your offices to discuss and sign cleaning contracts. If this is likely to happen, you should have an office space.

Choosing a business a location in the heavily populated downtown retail centre works both ways. Not only will your prospects have trouble-free access to your offices, but you'll also benefit by not having to travel long distances to get to most, if not all of your clients. This may not sound a big deal, but the cost in gas-saving and in your daily transportation needs will certainly increase your profit margins.

## Other Factors for Choosing a Business Location

There are several other factors you have to consider when choosing a business location for your cleaning company:

### i. Pedestrian Heavy Locations:

The side attraction of this choice is that people observe your brand on an almost daily basis, and they start to recognize you and talk about you. This works exceedingly well down the road bringing you word of mouth advertising and more leads as a result.

### ii. Hired staff and Storage Space:

If you plan on hiring employees, make sure you take that into account when choosing a business location. Your office will be spacious enough space to house your employees. Ideally, you'll want to plan ahead of the strength of your operation in the near future when choosing a business location so that you do not have to move when your business grows. If you're using company vehicles to convey your employees and equipment to client locations, you may also need to consider having a parking spot.

**iii. Proximity to Competitors:**

Selecting a business location that is close to competitor companies isn't always a bad idea. If the market is large, it shouldn't be a problem at all. If however, the market is small and your competition is already known in that market, you should probably be looking for alternative locations unless you have every reason to compete favourably. Competition can keep you vigilant and compel you to improve your services, and become more cost-effective, implement new marketing strategies etc.

With the above, together with the local government suggestion, you will be in a position to make informed decisions when making a choice of your cleaning business office location.

# CHAPTER TWELVE:

# Marketing tips

Cleaning business is worthwhile if you have the zeal and drive to build it into a profitable business you can. It doesn't really matter what size of the cleaning business it is, the fundamentals are the same. Here are a few thoughts to get the juices flowing

• Have a systematic approach that ensures every job your business does is thorough, meets the specific requirements of your client and it is done with a high level of care. People will notice your organization going the extra mile to put away breakables of small objects or dangerous equipment out of harm's way before starting, for instance..

• Differentiate yourself by studying products and techniques that will show that you know your "craft". This may be things like environmentally (and especially a pet) friendly cleaning substances, free from toxic, non-scratch cloths, tools to easily reach difficult surfaces etc. It may need extra investment, but all you need is one or two clients to notice it and the word will spread.

• Try to come up with "little extras" that can really set you apart. I am thinking of something like leaving a quality gift token with a hand-written thank you card on a table once the job is completed. It's amazing what a little extra of this kind will do for your relationship with your clients.

• Make sure that every customer is treated equally well even if they do not appear responsive to your apparent friendly approach. Your happy customers will be your best promotional tool.

• Put in place a system of follow up after the job is done to get feedback on the customer's experience. Deal with negative feedback fast and with every sense of responsibility.

• If you have employees, take care of them well. They are the ambassadors of your business and their attitude, work ethic and thoughtfulness will make or mar your business. They need to be favourably paid, encouraged, trained and, most importantly, must feel as though they have a stake in the business success which is more than just a paycheck at the end of the week.

• Very importantly, monitor your cash flow, only borrow when is absolutely necessary and as little as possible and manage your assets and liabilities well. No matter how well you're doing on the front line, if the business itself is not well managed, it's is only a question of time, it will go burst. In a business of this nature, don't forget to insure potential damage to customer possessions. Breaking an expensive bud vase could send you're your business to an early grave and land you in hot water.

• This kind of business should compete against competitors on price - it's a zero-sum game. It is advisable to focus more on a premium (but still affordable) service by offering superior service considered better than most of your competition.

• It is a good idea if you are online (with a website possibly) and encourage customers to rate your service on sites like Yelp. If you get a bad review, make sure you deal with it in a professional manner. It is possible your competitors will try to slag you off by submitting false negative reviews, especially if you snatch business away from them, but every harmful review is a golden moment to show how you can handle bad situations, which will reward you positively in the long run.

• Finally; in situations where people can phone you for emergency cleanups, where, for example, their kids have spilt vegetable oil all over the kitchen floor or have caused a flood in the apartment by leaving the tap on for a long time. They can contact you and you can send someone out to clean the mess up. It cost would need to be carefully calculated so it's not unreasonably expensive,

but if well-executed, you have registered
your name in that house for good.

Cleaning businesses are very alike from
hands-on experience. By taking the bold step
to stand out on one hand and controlling
your budget on the other, there is no reason
that you couldn't build your business into a
very successful and profitable enterprise.